SIGHT

HEARING

TOUCH

TASTE

SMELL

VESTIBULAR

PROPRIOCEPTION

This is Gabriel Making Sense of School © 2010

Copyright Hartley Steiner © 2010
Illustrations by Brandon Fall, www.fallillustration.com
All rights reserved.
Printed in North America.
No part of this publication may be reproduced in whole or in part, or stored in a retrieval system, or transmitted in any form or by any means, electronic, mechanical, photocopying, recording, or otherwise, without the written permission of the author, Hartley Steiner.
ISBN: 978-1-4269-2777-5

Library of Congress Control Number: 2010902142

Order this book online at www.trafford.com
or email orders@trafford.com
Most Trafford titles are also available at major online book retailers.

Trafford rev. 2/16/2010

www.trafford.com
North America & international
toll-free: 1 888 232 4444 (USA & Canada)
phone: 250 383 6864 ♦ fax: 812 355 4082

Dedicated to my husband Jeff for standing strong with me through the ups and downs of raising our kids, to my sons Gabriel, Nicholas, & Matthew for being the most amazing boys in this whole wide world, and to Stuart and Helen for proving time and time again there is no limit to their love for all of us. HS

Dedicated to my sister Rachelle, who has always enjoyed children and chose a career working with children with special needs. BF

THIS IS GABRIEL

MAKING SENSE OF SCHOOL

A BOOK ABOUT SENSORY PROCESSING DISORDER

WRITTEN BY HARTLEY STEINER
ILLUSTRATED BY BRANDON FALL

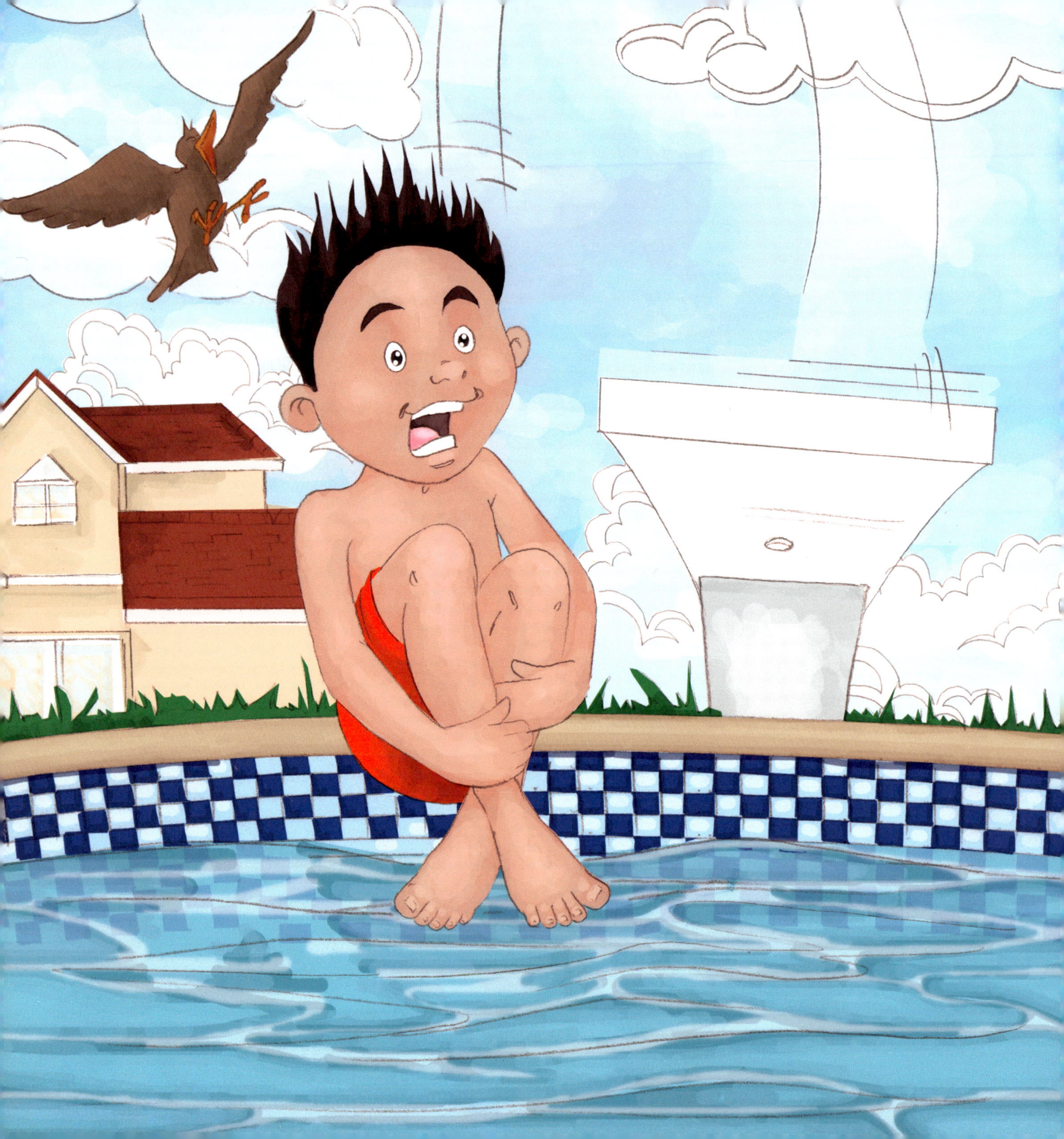

This is Gabriel. Gabriel is super funny, loves to ride his bike, and can make the biggest cannonball splash you have ever seen! Gabriel also has Sensory Processing Disorder (SPD). That is a long name for saying that his brain doesn't understand what his senses are telling it which often causes him to react inappropriately.

There are 7 sensory systems: *Sight, Hearing, Touch, Taste, Smell, Vestibular and Proprioception.*

Each one of these senses is responsible for telling you about the world around you and is necessary for making your body function during the day. For kids with SPD, all of the information from their senses gets jumbled up and they just can't figure out how to react. There are many kids that have this problem; Gabriel is just one of them.

This is Gabriel making sense of school.

SIGHT

Your eyes are used for sight and help you to see.

At school kids use their sense of sight to see lots of things, like a smile on someone's face or the artwork on the wall. But being able to see someone's smile or to focus on one piece of artwork is difficult for Gabriel.

There are lots of kinds of smiles—from a BIG super happy smile to a little shy smile; they are all different. Most kids with SPD have a hard time telling them apart. Not understanding the meaning behind the look on someone's face makes it hard for kids with SPD respond appropriately to their friends and teachers at school.

There are also times when Gabriel is in a classroom with so many things to look at; he can't pick out just one. At school it can be hard to focus on your school work or the teacher when there are just too many other things to look at.

Gabriel learns best when there are fewer things on the walls and teachers to help him through social situations that he may misinterpret.

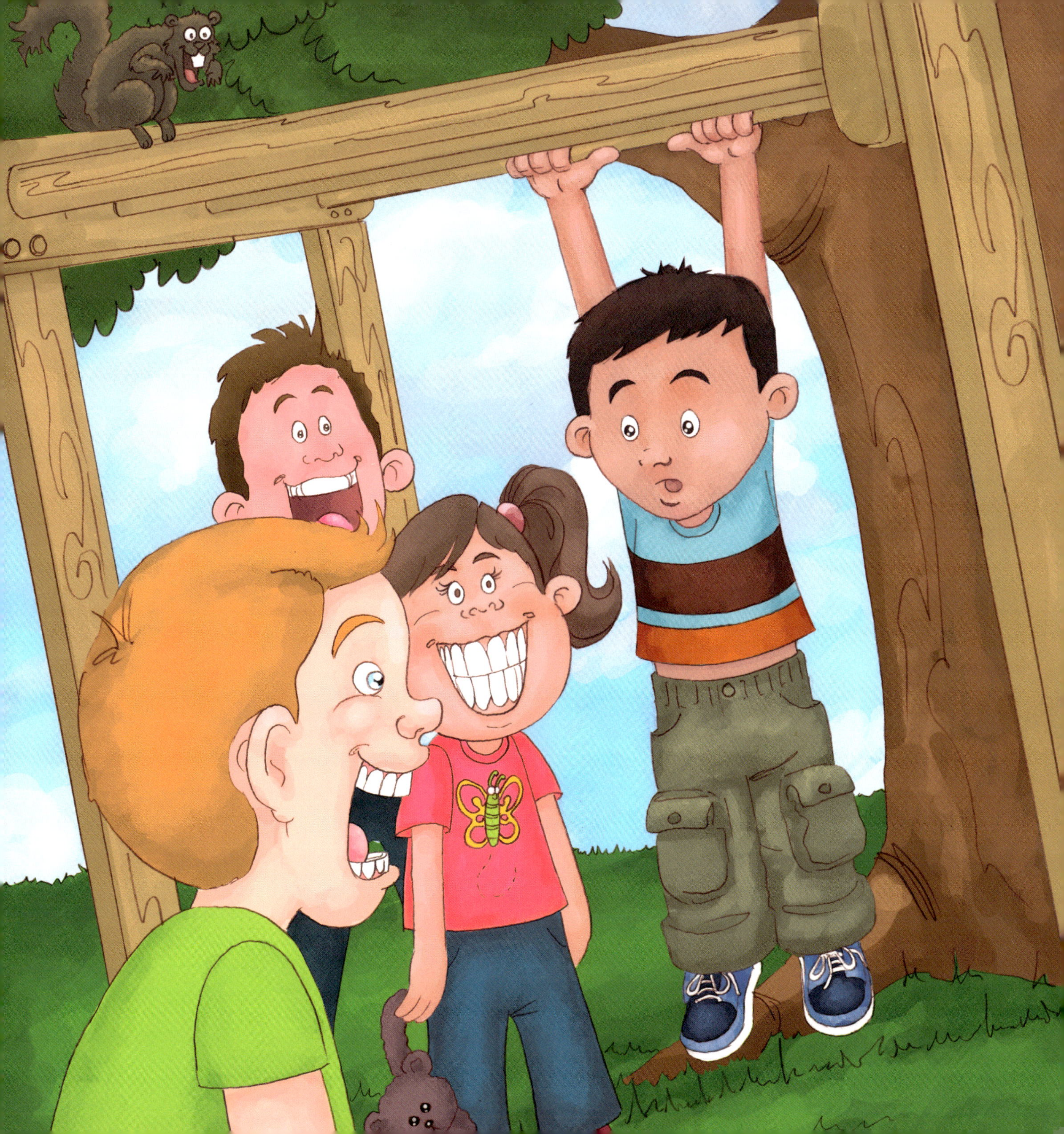

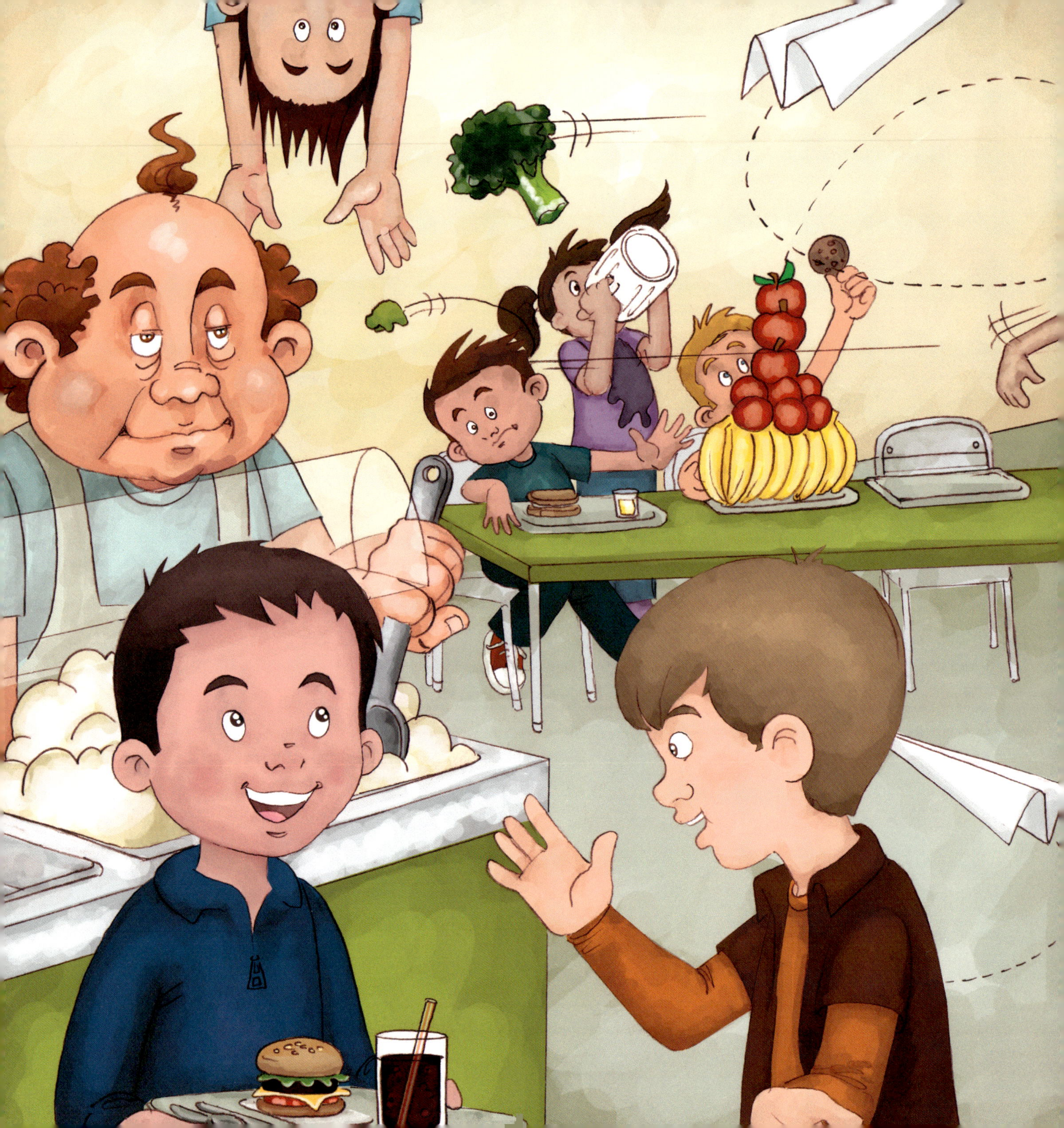

HEARING

Your ears are used to help you hear.

Gabriel can feel super overwhelmed by noise at school. When the fire alarm goes off, especially without warning, Gabriel's ears hurt so badly that he has to cover them with his hands. It is too much sound for him.

Lunch in the cafeteria can be the worst. So many people talking, walking around and squeaking their chairs as they stand up makes for a loud room. How can Gabriel possibly talk with a friend when he just can't get the background noise out of his head?

Most days Gabriel spends his energy trying *not* to listen to things—ignoring the humming of the lights, the footsteps in the hallway, or the squeaking of the chairs.

Gabriel learns best when he has a quiet space to focus or he is provided with noise canceling headphones to help him concentrate.

TOUCH

Your fingers and skin are used for touch and help you feel.

Gabriel likes to touch lots of things. Some kids with SPD don't like to touch anything. Gabriel likes to touch things just to see how they feel. He might dig in the dirt at recess, or he may like to play with clay during group time to keep his fingers busy. Other kids with SPD might absolutely hate the idea of touching clay or anything dirty, each kid is different.

Many kids with SPD like to wear the same clothes every day because they are the only ones that are "soft" enough against their skin. Having an irritating tag in their shirt or wearing clothing that is not "just right" makes it super hard for kids with SPD to focus in class. Comfortable clothing is a must for kids with SPD.

Gabriel learns best when he has something to keep his hands busy. Fidget toys and manipulatives are great for helping Gabriel focus at school.

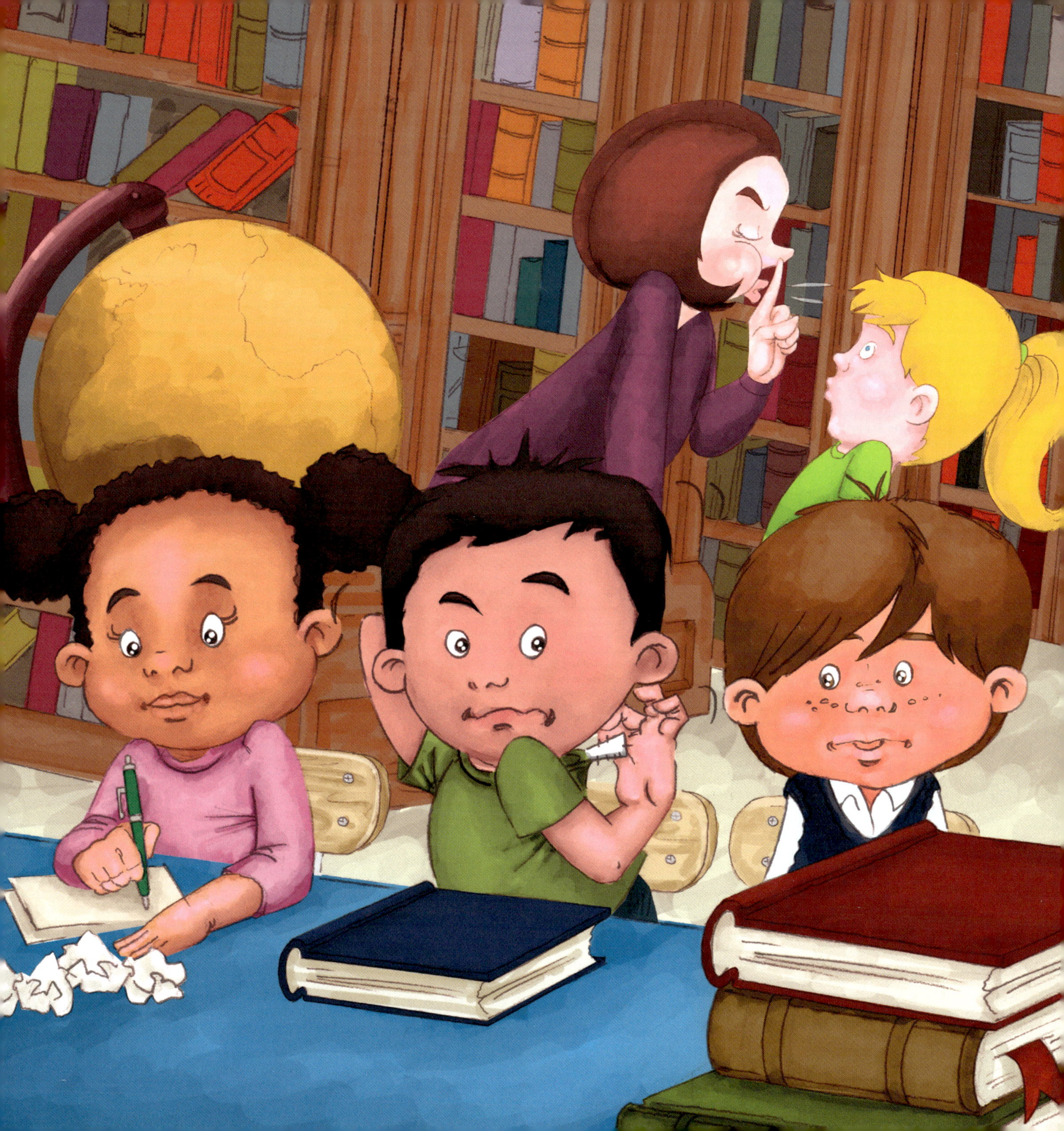

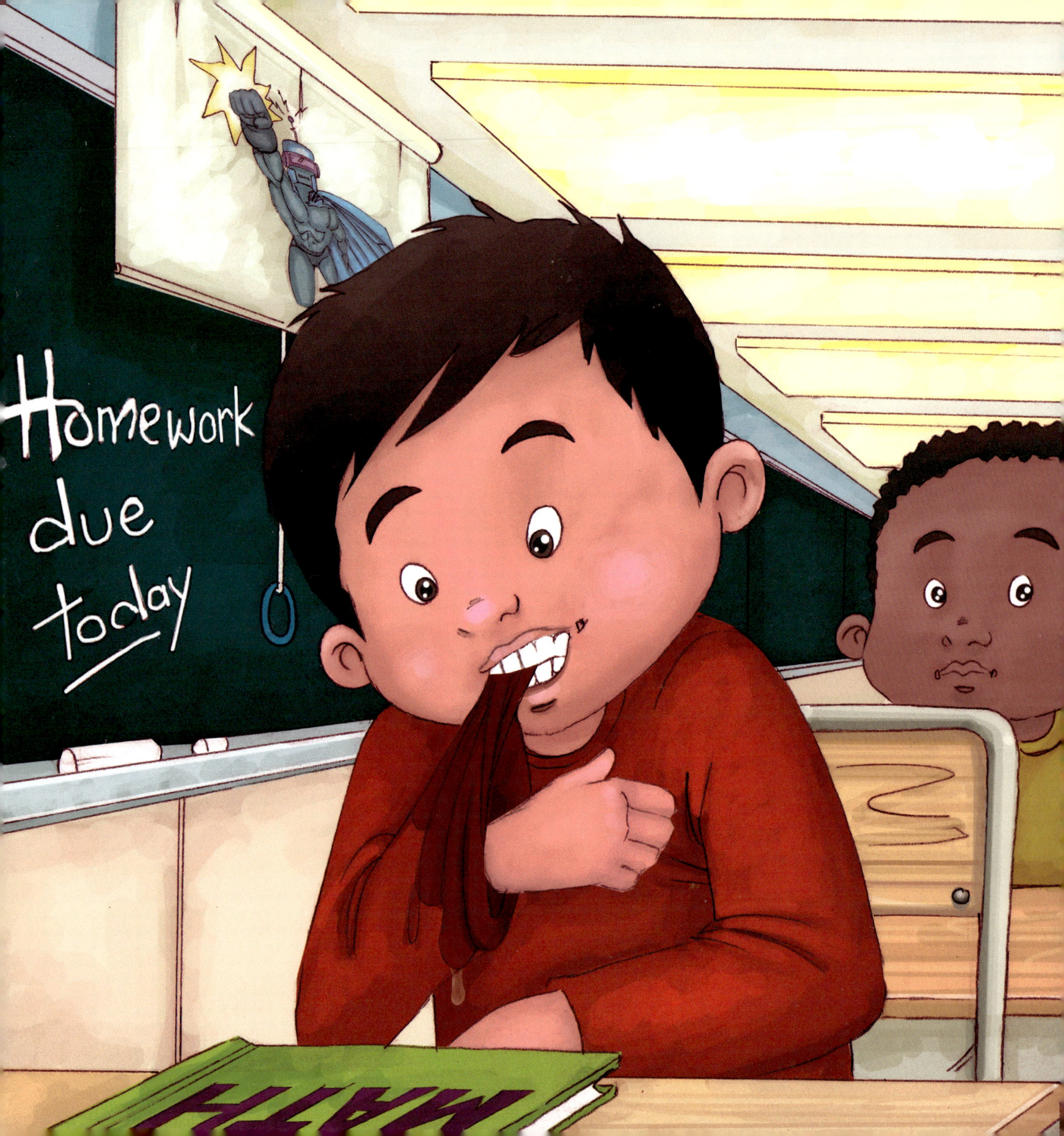
Homework
due
today
MATH

TASTE

Your mouth and tongue are used to help you taste.

Gabriel loves many different kinds of foods with lots of textures. He likes crunchy pretzels, soft creamy yogurt, and chewy fruit snacks. His favorite foods are spicy like hot salsa and Thai curry.

But, since all kids with SPD are different, there are some kids that like only a few foods. Plain foods like chicken nuggets and macaroni and cheese are common favorites for kids with SPD.

Often kids with SPD put things in their mouth that are not food too. Like chewing the end of a pencil or having the sleeve of their shirt in their mouth all day long until it is soaking wet. At school, some kids with SPD chew on gum to help them focus on their work and to remind them not to chew their clothing or anything else.

Gabriel learns best when he is able to chew gum, or when he has something else safe to chew on like a water bottle.

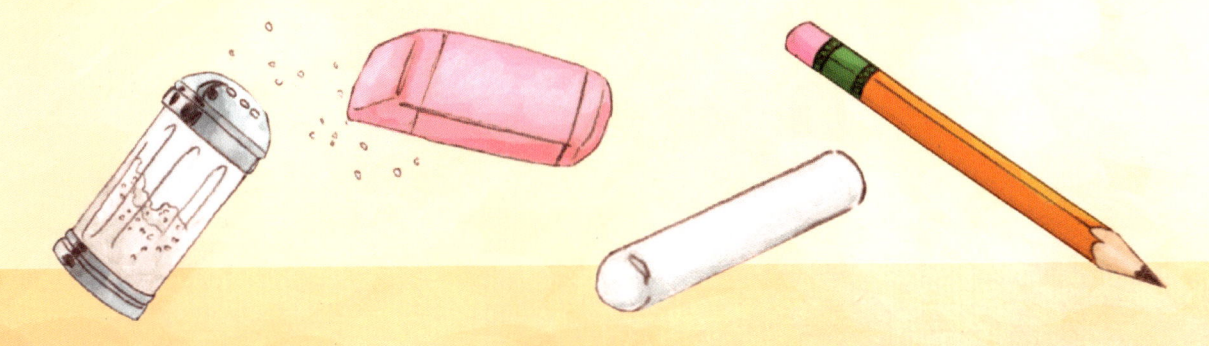

SMELL

Your nose is used to help you smell.

At school there are lots of smells that most people don't notice, but Gabriel does!

Sometimes he does not like smells that other people think are OK. Kids with SPD might feel grossed out when they smell all kinds of foods, soaps, lotions, and other smells that are around them every day. Some days Gabriel can feel the opposite too—and want to smell everything—even the markers.

When you have SPD and are trying to get your school work done, a bad smell can be really distracting.

Gabriel learns best when there are no strong smells around him.

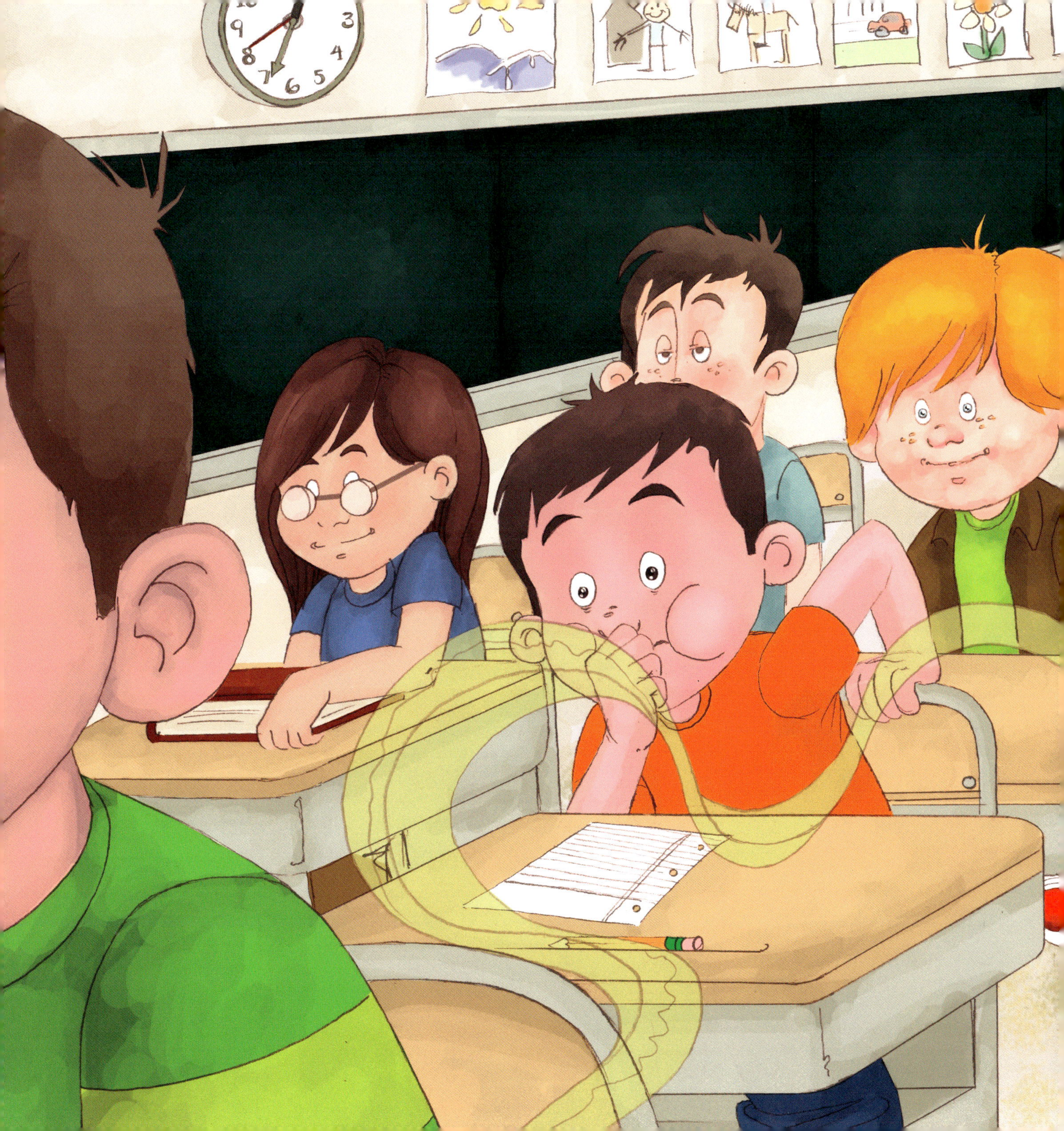

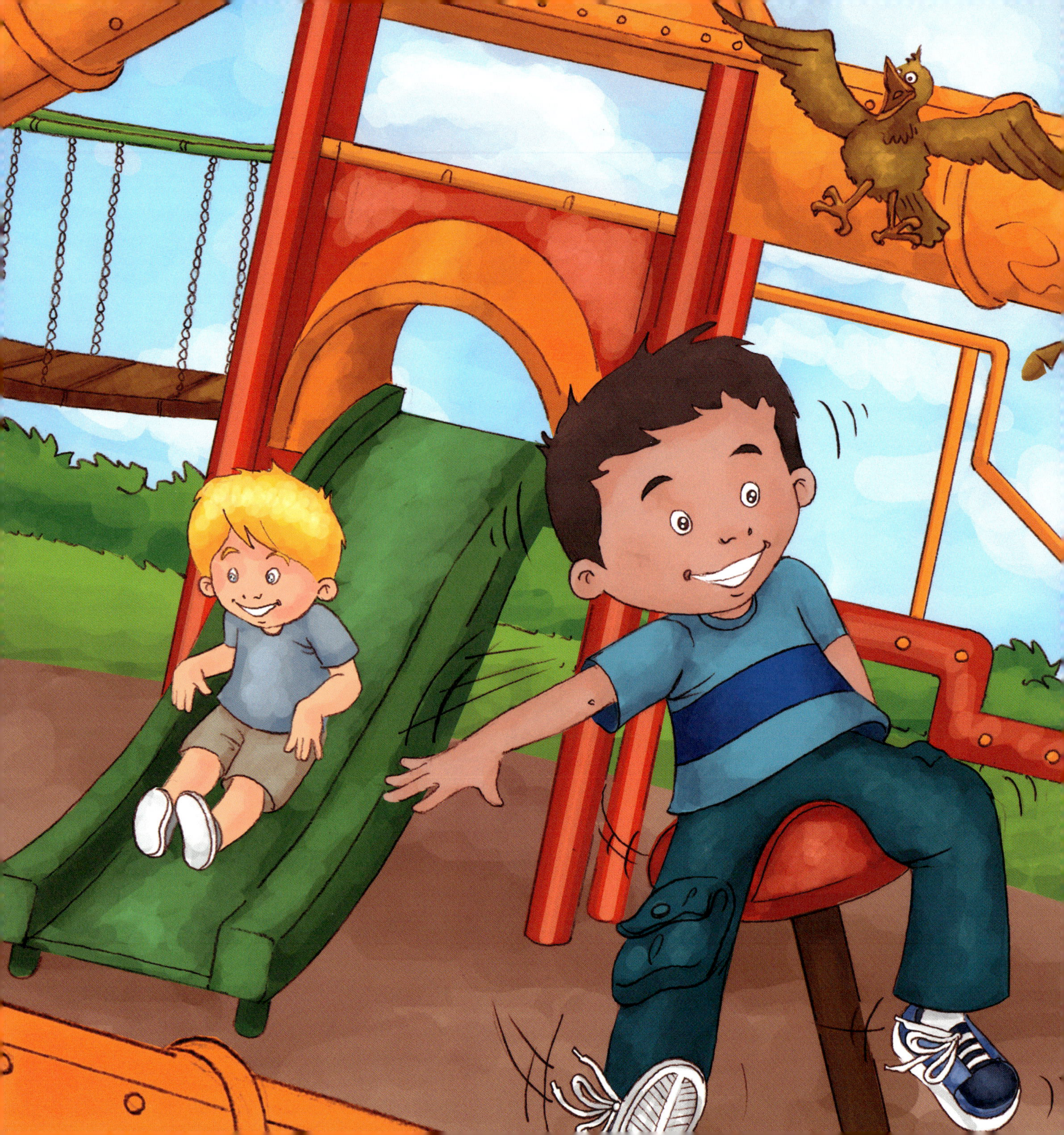

VESTIBULAR

Your inner ear is used to help you balance which is your vestibular sense.

Some kids with SPD may be clumsy. They may just fall out of their chair for no reason or seem to trip on nothing at all. At school it is hard to keep seated or play on the playground without falling for these kids.

Other kids, like Gabriel, may be able to climb to the tippy top of the jungle gym with no problems. Every kid is different.

You may see Gabriel spinning around and around during recess, trying to get what his body needs to keep working for the rest of the day.

Gabriel learns best when he can keep his body moving. His teacher gives him the opportunity to have "sensory breaks" which allows him to get up and walk around through the day.

PROPRIOCEPTION

Your sense of proprioception is in your joints and muscles. It is used to help you push and pull things.

Gabriel loves to push and pull things; it helps to keep his body feeling calm and organized. Something that is very important for him if he is going to learn at school.

It can be hard for kids with SPD to get their work done, because sitting in their desks for even a short amount of time can feel impossible some days. Kids like Gabriel may rest their feet on a large rubber band wrapped around the legs of their chair, use a weighted pad on their lap while they work at their desk or they may just choose to stand instead of sit.

Gabriel learns best when he is given opportunities to do "heavy work" during the school day. Pulling the lunch wagon, re-shelving tubs of books, or even just helping wipe down the tables after lunch allows him to get the proprioceptive work out his body needs.

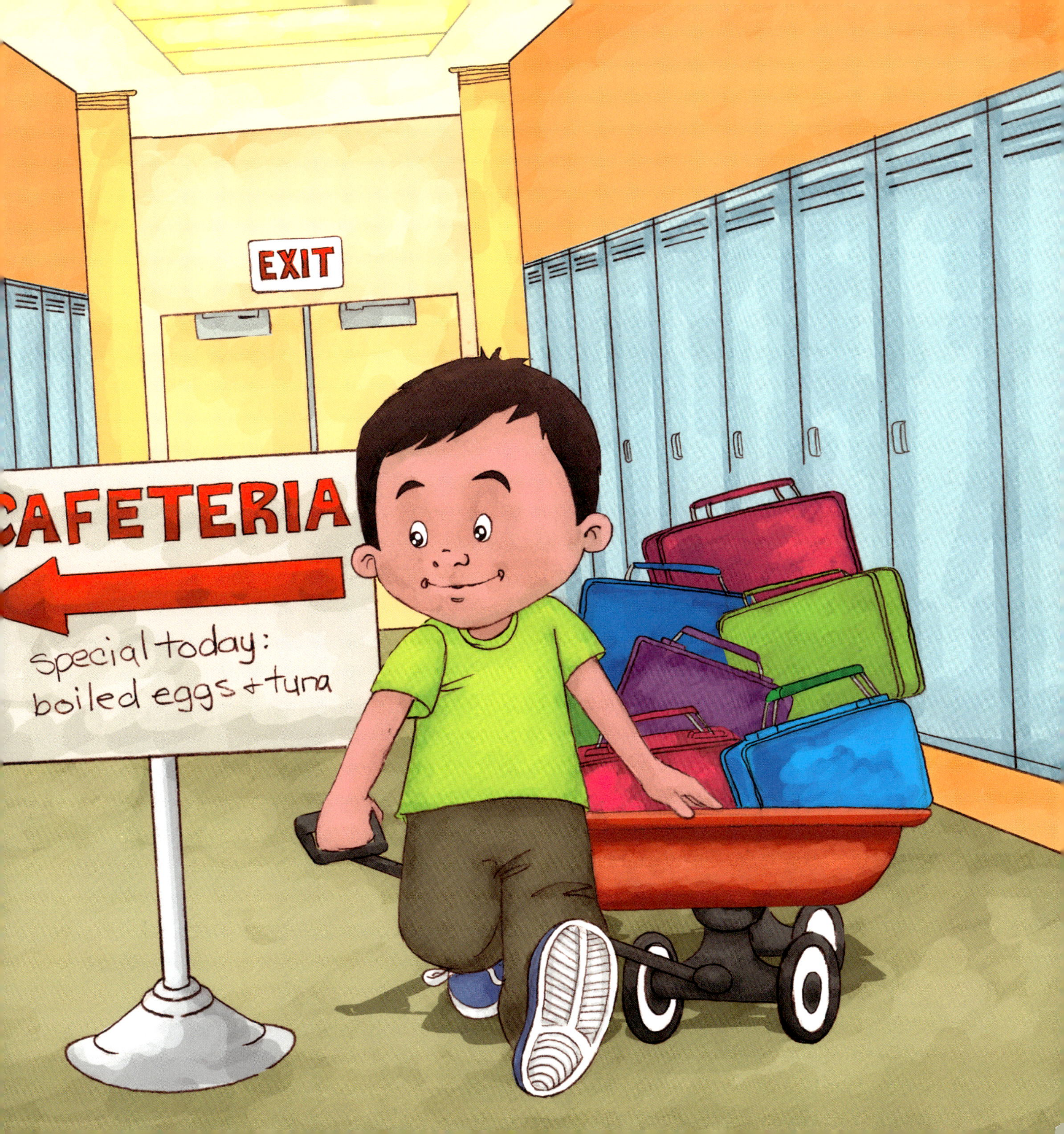
EXIT
CAFETERIA
special today:
boiled eggs + tuna

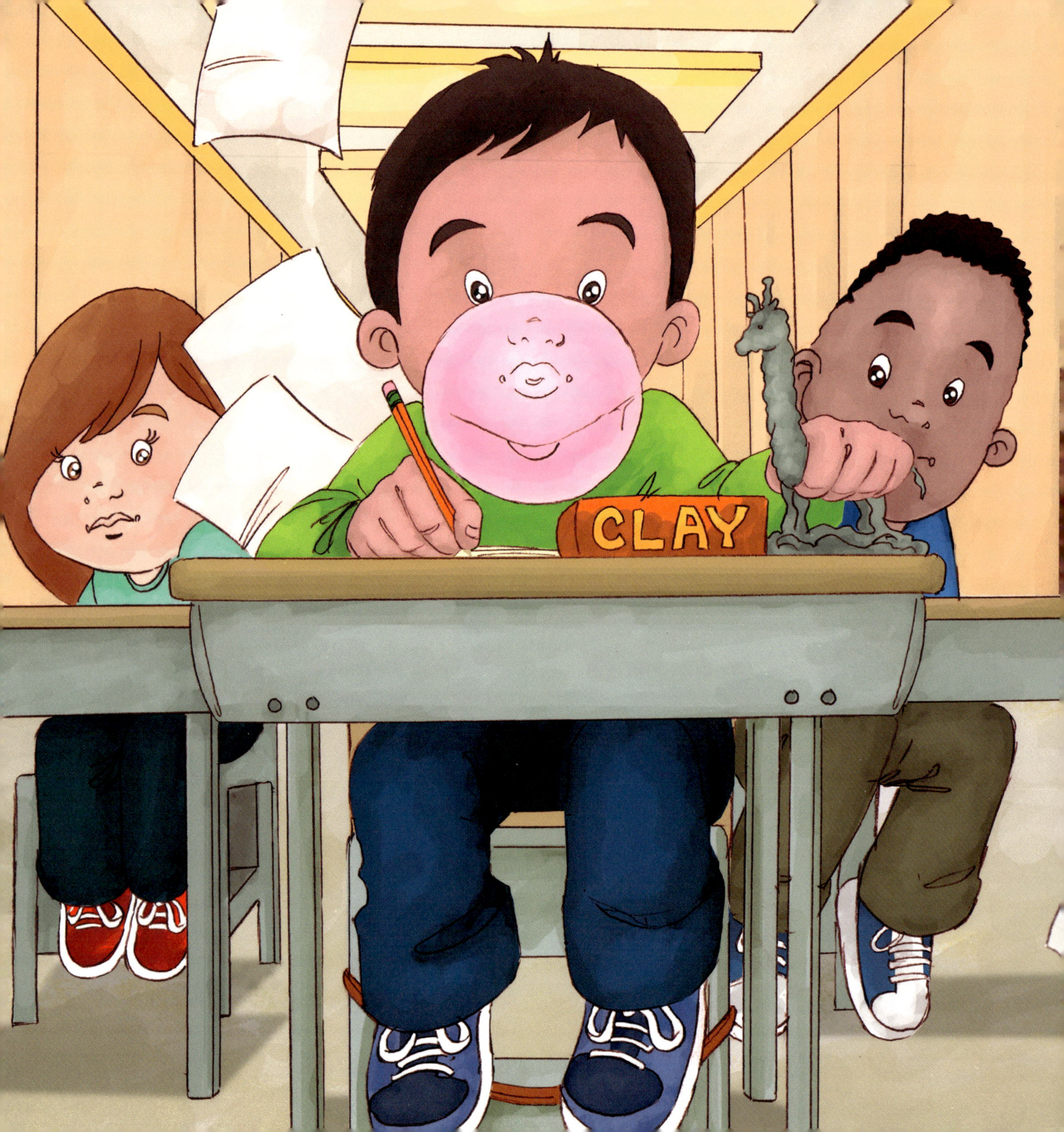
CLAY

As you can see, school can be an exhausting place for Gabriel, and all kids with Sensory Processing Disorder. With all the work it takes to keep their bodies calm and organized, it is amazing that they ever have time to learn anything! All kids with Sensory Processing Disorder need help managing their sensory needs at school.

Having understanding friends, an educated teacher and a support staff made up of Occupational Therapists, School Counselors and other specialists that are familiar with SPD is key for every child struggling with Sensory issues.

Gabriel loves to learn—and he has many accommodations at school that allow him to get his sensory needs met, making him a learning sensation!

Important Information for Parents, Educators, and Therapists:

Sensory Processing Disorder is growing each year. Currently the SPD Foundation in Denver, Colorado is estimating that as many as 1 in 20 children have sensory symptoms significant enough to hurt their social, emotional and academic development. It is important to educate ourselves and others about how sensory differences affect millions of children.

Whether you are a parent, educator or therapist, your help is needed to keep kids with SPD learning in the classroom!

There are many simple things you can do for the children in your care including giving sensory breaks, providing "quiet space" for children to calm down (under a desk or in a quiet corner), offering options for standing, or sitting on a ball at their desks, providing a weighted lap pad, pencil grips, and opportunities to get proprioceptive input through "heavy work".

If you need more simple ideas on what you can do to help your child in the classroom, go to www.hartleysboys.com to download a free list of sensory accommodations for the classroom specifically created by Hartley Steiner with help from her son Gabriel's Occupational Therapist, Kelly Flemetakis, OTR/L.

For More Information on SPD Visit

www.spdfoundation.net – The SPD Foundation is the world's leader on SPD research. Their site offers invaluable online learning plus information on seminars and an annual symposium. You can also search to find your local Parent Connections Support Group for parents and caregivers of sensational children.

www.sensoryplanet.com – Sensory Planet is a social networking site dedicated to SPD. The site offers families, educators and therapists working with sensational kids a place to share information and find online support.

www.hartleysboys.com – Hartley Steiner's personal blog chronically her life raising a child with SPD as well as two others while trying to keep her sanity and sense of humor.

About the Author:

Hartley Steiner lives in the Seattle area with her husband Jeff and their three sons: Gabriel, Nicholas and Matthew. Her oldest son Gabriel was diagnosed with Sensory Processing Disorder in 2005, just months before his adoption from Foster Care was finalized, opening a new chapter in her life. Since then she has become a dedicated advocate, not just for her own son, but for the millions of other children affected by Sensory Processing Disorder (SPD). Hartley spends her days at home chasing all three boys and chronicling the never ending chaos that is her life on the blog Hartley's Life With 3 Boys (www.hartleysboys.com). This is her first children's book, which she hopes will be of many, designed to promote awareness and understanding of Sensory Processing Disorder.

About the Illustrator:

Brandon Fall has always loved illustration and spent countless hours of his childhood getting lost in his drawings. He is now fortunate to make a living continuing to do what he loves from his home in the Rocky Mountains in Colorado. He enjoys spending time with his wife Lynette and his daugher Caitlyn in the beautiful outdoors. You can see more of his work at www.fallillustration.com.

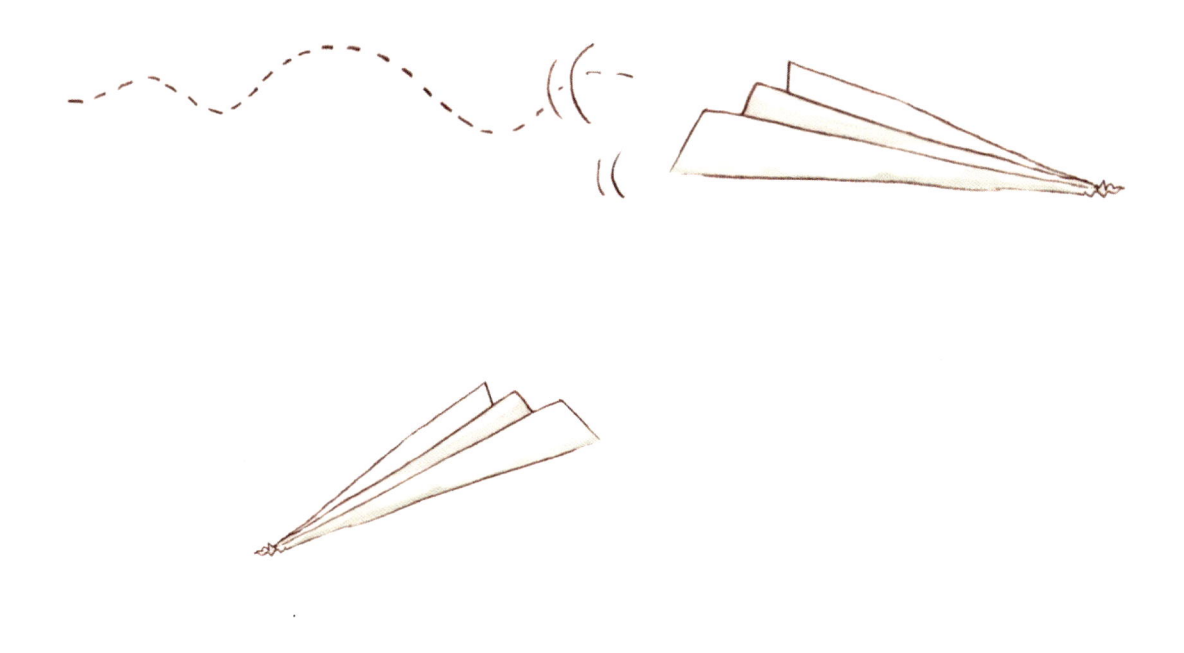

LaVergne, TN USA
06 September 2010
196014LV00003B